D1209474

WORLD'S
BIGGEST
REPTILES

Thanks to the creative team:
Senior Editor: Alice Peebles
Fact checking: Tim Harris
Designer: www.mayermedia.co.uk

Hungry Tomato®
A division of Lerner Publishing Group, Inc.
241 First Avenue North
Minneapolis, MN 55401 USA

For reading levels and more information, look up
this title at www.lernerbooks.com.

Main body text set in Calisto MT 12.5/14.5.
Typeface provided by Monotype Typography.

Library of Congress Cataloging-in-Publication Data

Names: Jackson, Tom, 1972– author. | Jevtic, Vladimir,
illustrator.
Title: World's biggest reptiles / Tom Jackson ; [illustrator]
Vladimir Jevtic.
Description: Minneapolis : Hungry Tomato, [2018] | Series:
Extreme reptiles | Audience: Ages 8–12. | Audience: Grades
4 to 6. | Includes index. | Identifiers: LCCN 2018004246
(print) | LCCN 2018005445 (ebook) | ISBN 9781541523876
(eb pdf) | ISBN 9781541500914 (lb : alk. paper)
Subjects: LCSH: Reptiles—Miscellanea—Juvenile literature. |
Reptiles—Size—Juvenile literature.
Classification: LCC QL644.2 (ebook) | LCC QL644.2
.J33275 2018 (print) | DDC 597.902—dc23

LC record available at https://lccn.loc.gov/2018004246

Manufactured in the United States of America
1-43760-33620-3/27/2018

World's
BIGGEST
REPTILES

by Tom Jackson
Illustrated by Vladimir Jevtic

HUNGRY
TOMATO®

Minneapolis

CONTENTS

MIGHTY REPTILES

Prepare to meet some of the biggest reptiles out there. Some are truly immense beasts, such as the mighty saltwater crocodile, green anaconda, and leatherback turtle, which make us look very small in comparison. Others are simply the largest of their kind, such as the mischievous tokay gecko of Southeast Asia, or the biggest in their local part of the world, such as Africa's Gaboon viper.

A muscular green anaconda on the lookout for prey

The insect-exterminating tokay gecko, often a welcome guest in human homes

The saltwater crocodile, a ferocious prowler of the seas and rivers

REASONS TO BE BIG

The most obvious reason for an animal to be big is to be stronger than its enemies. For example, crocodiles are large so they can out-swim and out-bite their prey and fend off (almost) any attack. However, being big is also a way of saving energy. Small animals warm up fast but cool down quickly as well. A larger body holds onto its heat for longer, and so needs less food, relative to its size, to keep working. This drive for efficiency is why many reptiles, such as the leatherback turtle, have grown so large.

ISLAND GIANTS

Several giant reptiles—from hefty, domed tortoises to rough and tough iguanas—grew large on islands. This is down to a process called island gigantism, where animals that are normally small when living alongside a wide range of other animals—including big ones like deer, giraffes and tigers—find themselves alone on remote islands. As a result, they evolve to fill the place left by the missing large animals and grow huge in the process.

The giant Aldabra tortoise of the Seychelles Islands in the Indian Ocean

OCEAN SOFTIE

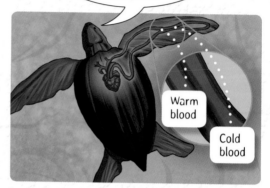

"The warm blood from my body heats up the cold blood from my flippers. Neat, huh?"

"Your stings don't bother me."

"Gulp!"

"Warm blood"

"Cold blood"

Leatherbacks swim into much colder water than other sea turtles. They have a clever heat swap system in their flippers to keep their body warm.

"The moon is big now, and it will be big again when the babies hatch."

Leatherbacks are specialist jellyfish feeders. Their throats are lined with spikes that burst the slimy, bag-shaped animals as they're swallowed. Otherwise the jellies would get stuck and choke the turtle.

Adult male leatherbacks always stay at sea, but the females come ashore at night when it's time to lay eggs on the beach. Often, they emerge from the ocean when there is a bright, full moon.

"I've made my nest above the high tide mark so the eggs will always stay dry."

"This way, everyone!"

"Follow the moon!"

The turtle is a great swimmer, but is clumsy on land. She works hard to dig a hole in the sand with her flippers and lays about 110 eggs.

The babies hatch after two months in the warm sand. They climb out, usually at night, and head away from the dark land toward the bright ocean.

LEATHERBACK TURTLE

The leatherback is the largest sea turtle of all. It is about as long as a double bed, but much wider. With its flippers outstretched, the turtle is nearly 10 feet (3 m) across. As its name suggests, the leatherback does not have a hard shell of bone as most other turtles and tortoises do. Instead, the animal is covered by a thick, rubbery skin stretched over a frame of rib bones. The lightweight, boat-shaped shell helps the turtle stay afloat and save energy as it swims.

LEATHERBACK TURTLE
DERMOCHELYS CORIACEA
Lifespan: more than 100 years
Size: 7 feet 2 inches (2.2 m)

HIGH SPEED
The leatherback is also the fastest reptile. It has been clocked swimming at 22.25 mph (35.28 km/h), seven times faster than a human swimmer. Usually other turtles swim much slower than this.

GOING DEEP
Leatherbacks can stay underwater for nearly 70 minutes and dive to more than 0.6 miles (1 km) below the surface. No other turtle goes so deep.

GIANT RELATIVE
The leatherback's prehistoric relative Archelon, from 80 million years ago, grew to twice the size and was the largest turtle ever to have lived.

ARMOR-PLATED

The giant tortoises of flat desert islands have "saddleback" shells. This shape allows the long-necked animals to reach up to leaves on tall bushes.

On islands with a mix of grass and shrubs, there live some very rare tortoises with flatter shells that are halfway between saddlebacks and domes.

Giant tortoises that live on mountainous islands covered in lush grass have domed shells. This shape protects the tortoises better as they munch away on grasses with their heads low to the ground.

A tiny group of giant tortoises lives on the Seychelles Islands in the Indian Ocean. These tortoises are almost as big as the Galápagos species and have much bumpier shells.

Giant tortoises are now very rare—thanks to humans. Sailors would catch them for food and even take a ride. The giants could survive on a ship for weeks, providing the crew with fresh meat. Sailors also brought goats to the tortoises' islands—which ate the plants. Today, all wild giant tortoises live on nature reserves.

GALÁPAGOS TORTOISE

The Galápagos giant tortoise is the largest species of land tortoise. Only sea turtles, which swim in the ocean rather than lumber on land, are larger. A giant tortoise is slow but solid. A big male can weigh three times as much as an adult human thanks to its thick, sturdy shell. The tortoise's shell is its only protection—it cannot run from danger because it has a top speed of 0.3 mph (0.5 km/h), slower than a toddler's crawl. However, the tortoises live on remote islands where the adults have no natural enemies. They grow so large not for defense but to be more efficient plant-eaters.

GALÁPAGOS TORTOISE
CHELONOIDIS NIGRA
Lifespan: 170 years
Size: 5 feet 10 inches (1.8 m)

SO LONELY
A Pinta giant tortoise called Lonesome George was once the rarest animal on Earth. From 1971 to his death in 2012, George was the last surviving member of his subspecies.

LAND OF THE TORTOISE
Most giant tortoises live on the Galápagos Islands in the Pacific Ocean. The islands are named after the Spanish word *galápago*, which means tortoise.

OCEAN ROVER

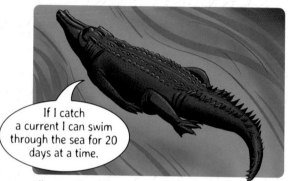

All crocodiles are expert swimmers, but the saltwater croc is the best of all. It can hit speeds of 15 mph (25 km/h) through the water, swishing its long tail for power and using its feet as rudders.

During the dry season when it is hard to find food on land, saltwater crocs head into the water. They swim from river mouths into the ocean, where they feed on fish and seabirds.

During the rainy season, saltwater crocs are more common inland. They attack animals that come down to drink on the banks of rivers and lakes. At this time, the crocodiles mate and lay eggs.

Salties cannot chew very well, so they swallow stones to grind up the food in their stomach. The stones also make the croc heavier so it can dive more easily.

The females bury their eggs in dry ground. Eggs laid in the middle of the nest produce males; eggs at the warmer top and colder bottom become females.

Like all reptiles, salties never stop growing, so older crocs are the largest—usually over twice human size, with some reportedly being over 33 feet (10 m) long.

SALTWATER CROCODILE

The largest reptile of all is the saltwater crocodile. This monster lives in the waters between Australia and India, around the many islands where the Indian and Pacific Oceans meet. There are many big animals that attack humans—mostly in self-defense—but very few that actually see us humans as food. The saltwater croc, or saltie, is the biggest and most dangerous of these. Every year about 100 people are attacked by a saltie—and half of them end up as the immense reptile's next meal.

SALTWATER CROCODILE
CROCODYLUS POROSUS
Lifespan: 70 years
Size: 23 feet (7 m)

KEEP AWAY
Saltwater crocodiles like to be alone and defend the territory around them. They attack other crocs that get too close—and anything else, even boats, that stray into their area.

BIG HEAD
A saltie's massive head alone weighs about 440 pounds (200 kg), which is about three times as heavy as an adult human. All that weight comes from the huge muscles used for biting.

MUSCLES AND MOUTH

The green anaconda does not kill with venom but squeezes, or constricts, its prey to death. The snake squeezes ever tighter with its coiled body each time its prey breathes out, finally suffocating it.

Once the prey is dead (or nearly dead), the snake starts to swallow it—head first. The snake's wind pipe opens at the front of the mouth, not down the throat, so it can breathe even when its mouth is full.

Every meal is swallowed whole, and the anaconda's body stretches to fit it in. It has very powerful stomach acid for dissolving its food—bones and all.

Female green anacondas are much larger than males. In the mating season, a dozen males coil around one female, making a ball of snakes—for a whole month!

Scientific studies of anacondas in the wild show that females grow to about 16 feet (5 m). They could swallow two people in a row!

In 2014, US TV naturalist Paul Rosolie tried to get eaten by an anaconda—and film it. He called for rescue just as the snake was biting his head.

GREEN ANACONDA

The green anaconda of the wetlands and rainforests of South America is the mightiest snake on Earth. It is not the longest snake, but it is the heaviest. An adult weighs at least 220 pounds (100 kg), which is more than an adult man. However, the snake is much stronger than us. The name anaconda comes from an Indian-language term that means "elephant killer." There are no elephants in South America for these big snakes to kill, but they prey on all animals, including other hunters, such as caimans, and even jaguars!

GREEN ANACONDA
EUNECTES MURINUS
Lifespan: 10 years
Size: 26 feet (8 m)

WATER SNAKE
Anacondas spend most of their time swimming in shallow water. The water supports their massive bodies, making it easier for them to move around.

BIG BABIES
Green anacondas give birth to their babies, rather than laying eggs. The newborns are already 24 inches (60 cm) long and one mother snake produces 40 at a time!

FEARSOME FANGSTER

The Gaboon viper is a master of disguise. It has a pale stripe down its back, which gives it a snake shape but makes it look like a much smaller species to any animals that spot it.

The snake's head looks like a wide, triangular arrowhead. This shape creates space on either side for the snake's massive venom glands, which pump out liquid poison during a bite.

The Gaboon viper's fangs are 2 inches (5 cm) long. They pump out 0.34 fl. oz. of venom per bite—10 times more than most snakes.

The viper spends most of its time motionless on the ground, hidden among leaves. Its eyes look in opposite directions searching for approaching prey.

This big viper kills its prey with one bite. It clamps down its jaws and does not let go so that it can inject a big dose of venom. It holds onto the prey until it is definitely dead, and swallows it whole.

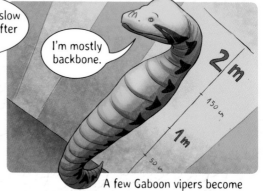

A few Gaboon vipers become longer than an adult man. The body is very wide compared to other snakes and gets its shape from more than 100 pairs of ribs. (Humans have 12.)

GABOON VIPER

The Gaboon viper of the rainforests of Central Africa is Africa's largest venomous snake. It has a maximum recorded weight of 26 pounds (12 kg). That might not sound like a lot, but when combined with the world's largest venom fangs, this chunky viper is a heavyweight hunter. Luckily for us, Africa's giant biter seldom attacks humans. Normally a warning is enough. The big snake produces a low, rhythmic hiss that sounds like a person gasping in and out for breath.

GABOON VIPER
BITIS GABONICA
Lifespan: 18 years
Size: 6 feet 6 inches (2 m)

ALL IN
Male Gaboon vipers engage in intense fights. They lift their heads and coil around each others' necks and then try to push their opponent over. They keep fighting even if they fall into a river!

EYES WIDE SHUT
The Gaboon viper spends a lot of time sleeping among the leaves. Like all snakes, it has no eyelids, so it cannot shut its eyes. Instead, the snake closes up its iris when asleep.

FOREST DRAGON

When they are young, rhino iguanas are small and agile enough to climb trees to find food. Older, heavier iguanas have to look for seeds and fruits that have fallen to the ground.

The seeds of many forest plants need to be eaten by an iguana before they can grow. The lizard's stomach digests away the seeds' hard outer coat, and the seeds sprout from the lizard's droppings.

The iguanas mate just before the rainy season. The males take over a patch of forest full of food to attract females. If a rival male turns up, the lizards have a show of strength. They lift up the spikes that run from head to tail and do push-ups and head bobs to scare off their rival—and impress any females watching.

The rhinoceros iguana gets its name from the rounded lumps on its nose. These are most obvious on older males, but females have them as well. The lumps reminded scientists of the nose horns on a rhinoceros. Unlike its mammal namesake, the iguana does not fight with its horns but uses them as a sign of strength.

RHINOCEROS IGUANA

The rhinoceros iguana is the largest lizard in North America. Like a lot of giant reptiles, such as the giant tortoise or Komodo dragon, this big lizard lives only on islands. Most of these tough iguanas live on Hispaniola, one of the largest Caribbean islands. Being cut off from the mainland, islands do not have a wide variety of animals. Until humans brought farm animals to Hispaniola, the plant-eating rhinoceros iguana was the biggest animal on the island.

RHINOCEROS IGUANA
CYCLURA CORNUTA
Lifespan: 20 years
Size: 4 feet 7 inches (1.4 m)

BIG BUILD
Rhino iguanas are not as long as their mainland relative, the green iguana, but they are much chunkier and twice as heavy, at 22 pounds (10 kg).

NATIVE NAME
The word "iguana" comes from the Taino language spoken by the people who lived on Hispaniola before European conquerors arrived.

Climbing Caller

The name "tokay" is a Malaysian word. It sounds like the squeaky but loud mating call made by male geckos. However, some people hear it differently and think its sounds like "hankok" or "pookay." In fact, the general term "gecko" also comes from this lizard's distinctive call.

The tokay's loud calling is meant to attract female mates. The male finds a high branch so it can be seen from all around. The call is also a warning to keep other males away. If that doesn't work, the males fight by biting each other's snouts. Ouch.

A tokay has a strong bite. It has little teeth for gripping onto prey, but it kills its food by crushing victims in its jaws. It only needs to eat a few times a week and does most of its hunting at night.

Like all lizards, the gecko regularly molts, or sheds its old skin, revealing a clean, healthy covering underneath. During the molt, the outer layer dries out and flakes off.

TOKAY

The tokay is the largest gecko in the world. It lives in the rainforests of Southeast Asia, clambering around the branches looking for insects to eat. Most geckos are small and slender, but the tokay is much chunkier and tougher. Even so, it is still an expert climber, using sticky pads on each of its toes to grip smooth leaves and bark. The lizard is bluish and covered in orange spots, which are brighter on the show-off males.

TOKAY
GEKKO GEKKO
Lifespan: 10 years
Size: 14 inches (35 cm)

COLOR SWITCH
Tokays can make themselves darker to absorb heat on cold days, and also become paler to blend in with their surroundings. Can you spot any hiding in the pictures?

DRAGON DESCENDANTS
Tokays are popular pets in eastern Asia, where people believe they bring good luck. The impressive lizards are said to be relatives of the mighty dragons that rule over nature.

DESERT THUG

The Gila monster spends almost all its time hidden in a burrow. It comes out early in the morning to find food. After rare desert rains, the monster is more active, often bathing in puddles.

Gila monsters are tough lizards that live for more than 20 years. They move with a lumbering walk, dragging their tail behind them. They move very slowly but just keep on going.

The lizard gives a strong bite with its long, spiked teeth. Its venom is not squirted out like a snake's, but drizzles out from a coating on the lower teeth.

It creeps up on its prey and bites by surprise. The monster latches on to victims for several minutes and waits for the venom to take effect.

The eggs of birds, snakes, and lizards are the monster's favorite food. It may climb up trees and cacti to raid nests. It can also sniff out eggs in underground nests and digs doggedly into the loose earth with its front legs to get at them. The greedy lizard can eat up to a third of its weight in one meal.

GILA MONSTER

The Gila monster—pronounced "HEE-luh"—is a burly desert hunter. It is the largest lizard living in the United States. The Gila monster is an unusual species with only one close relative left alive, the Mexican beaded lizard. Both these desert critters have rounded, studlike scales hardened with pieces of bone instead of overlapping scales like other lizards. Both have poisonous saliva, which kills their prey. The poison does not harm humans too much, but the monster can give a painful, nasty bite—if it can catch you!

GILA MONSTER
HELODERMA SUSPECTUM
Lifespan: 30 years
Size: 24 inches (60 cm)

FAT TAIL
Gila monsters need to survive long periods without food. They store up a supply of fat in their chubby tail to keep them going in the lean times.

BAD REP
The lizard is called "monster" because Native American myths say it is a deadly creature that can leap high into the air and kill just by breathing on you. Luckily, none of this is true.

SNAKE EAT SNAKE

Even other snakes are not safe from the king cobra. It occasionally eats rats and birds, but its main prey are other snakes. If anything, they are easier to eat!

The king cobra can lift the first third of its body off the ground. A long one can look a human right in the eye. It does this to scare away attackers, giving out a hiss so low that it sounds like a growl.

King cobras are most dangerous during the breeding season. The female buries her eggs under leaves and sits guard. She does not go off to hunt and attacks anything that comes too near.

The baby cobras hatch out after about 10 weeks in the nest. Just before they hatch, their mother slithers away fast. She is so hungry that she might start eating her own babies! The baby snakes are about 20 inches (50 cm) long—and already deadly. But their fangs are so short their bites would barely break the skin.

KING COBRA

The king cobra is the longest venomous snake in the world. It lives in the forests of eastern India and Southeast Asia. It is as long as a python and has a head the size of a man's hand. Its long fangs deliver a powerful venom that can kill an elephant. The snake's big bite pumps large amounts of the venom deep into the muscles of its victim. One bite can kill a person in less than 30 minutes.

KING COBRA
OPHIOPHAGUS HANNAH
Lifespan: 20 years
Size: 19 feet (5.8 m)

HUNTING THE HUNTERS
The mighty king of snakes prefers to be left alone, so it rarely bites humans. Most people who die from bites have gone into remote forests looking for the snake.

FURRY NEMESIS
The Indian mongoose is immune to the king cobra's venom and is therefore the snake's worst enemy, or nemesis. Pet mongooses help to keep deadly snakes away from homes.

Buzz Tail Rattlers

Rattlesnakes are very grumpy and aggressive snakes and are more likely to bite than most other more venomous snakes. They use their tail rattle and hiss loudly to scare off threats while coiling their body, ready to attack. They will also strike out at enormous speed. The snake can reach a target that is half its own body length away—and it can land a bite in less than a tenth of a second.

Rattlesnakes ambush their prey. They hide out in rocks, thickets, and even landfills—anywhere that rats and other favorite prey scurry around.

The rattler's dry bite is venom-free. When it wants to kill, it squeezes the venom glands behind its eyes to pump the poison through its hollow fangs.

The female gives birth to up to 25 babies in late summer. She stays with them for a few hours, until they go off to find food. She never sees them again.

The snake's rattle is made from balls of dried skin. New balls are added every time the snake sheds its skin, so older snakes have longer, louder rattles.

DIAMONDBACK RATTLESNAKES

The biggest venomous snakes in the United States are the diamondback rattlesnakes. The eastern diamondback of Florida and the Deep South is slightly longer and much chunkier than the western species, which lives in the deserts of the Southwest and Mexico. However, the western diamondback bites more Americans than any other snake, and together these rattlers kill about 12 people a year. The snake gets its name from the dark diamond shapes that curve over its back, divided from each other by paler stripes.

DIAMONDBACK RATTLESNAKES
CROTALUS SPECIES
Lifespan: 20 years
Size: 6 feet 10 inches (2.1 m)

STARVATION DIET
Rattlesnakes can go for two years without feeding. The snake stays alive by saving its energy and will barely move unless prey comes close.

HEAVYWEIGHT RECORD
The eastern diamondback is one of the heaviest venomous snakes in the world—if not the heaviest. It has been weighed at 33 pounds (15 kg), which is more than the Gaboon viper and king cobra.

WORLD'S SMALLEST REPTILES

Record-breaking reptiles can be small as well as big. The smallest reptiles in the world are harder to find and less well-known than the biggest ones—and they are much less dangerous. However, they are just as incredible.

Leaf chameleon

(*Brookesia micra*):
At 1.1 inches (29 mm) from nose to tail, this tiny chameleon from Madagascar shares the record for the smallest lizard—and the smallest reptile of all. During the day, it crawls through the dead leaves that litter the ground looking for tiny insects. Being small helps it to stay hidden. At night, the chameleon sleeps in a tree.

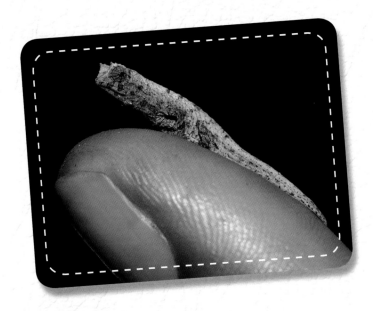

Cuvier's dwarf caiman

(*Paleosuchus palpebrosus*): This little caiman is the smallest of all the crocodilians (members of the crocodile family). It grows to just 4 feet (1.2 m) long, from its nose to the tip of its tail. It lives in clean, fast-flowing streams and rivers, where the water is too shallow for its larger cousins.

Barbados threadsnake (*Leptotyphlops carlae*): Just 4 inches (10 cm) long and looking a lot like a little earthworm, this tiny blind snake from the Caribbean island of Barbados survives by burrowing through the ground to find ants and other insects. The females lay only one egg each year. The egg is long and narrow, and about half the size of the mother.

Speckled padloper tortoise (*Homopus signatus*): Living in the dry meadows of South Africa and Namibia, this tortoise is the smallest of its kind. The females reach 4 inches (10 cm) long, which is 0.8 inches (2 cm) longer than the males. The cute little tortoises live among rocks, eating the small plants that grow around them.

EXTINCT GIANTS

Sarcosuchus (112 million years ago)

Twice as long as today's largest croc, this monster weighed 8.8 tons (8 t). It hunted just like a modern croc—only it preyed on dinosaurs.

Quetzalcoatlus (68 million years ago)

With a wingspan of 52 feet (16 m), this pterosaur was the largest flying animal ever. It soared over the plains looking for dead dinosaurs to eat.

Titanoboa (65 million years ago)

After the dinosaur era, snakes were the largest reptiles on Earth. *Titanoboa* was the largest ever: 45 feet (14 m) long and over 1.1 tons (1 t).

Mosasaurs (80 million years ago)

Distantly related to today's snakes and lizards, mosasaurs were immense ocean hunters. They grew to 55 feet (17 m) long and preyed on sharks.

Shonisaurus (215 million years ago)

The ichthyosaurs were ocean-going reptiles that looked like dolphins. *Shonisaurus* was the largest of the lot, at 49 feet (15 m) long. Icthyosaurs had the largest eyes in the animal kingdom to help them see in the gloomy water.

GLOSSARY

acid a chemical that attacks materials, breaking them down into simpler substances. Stomach juice contains strong acid.

aggressive ready or likely to attack without warning

efficiency a way of using fuel or energy without wasting much of it

gigantism a process that makes thing giant

glands body parts that produce important chemicals

intermediate halfway between one thing and another

mammal an animal that feeds its young on milk. Most mammals have hairy bodies.

myths old stories often involving made-up monsters and heroes

rib a curved bone that sticks out from the spine to give the middle of the body shape and strength

suffocate to die, or make something die, from being unable to breathe properly

territory a region or area controlled by one animal

venom a poison produced by an animal and pumped into prey or an attacker to kill them

wetland an area of land covered in shallow water for most of the year

windpipe the tube that connects the throat to the lungs

INDEX

The Author

Tom Jackson has written about 200 books over 25 years—his specialties are natural history, technology, and all things scientific. Tom studied zoology at Bristol University and has worked in zoos and as a conservationist. He's mucked out polar bears, surveyed in the Vietnamese jungle, and rescued wildlife from drought in Africa. Writing jobs have also taken him to the Galápagos Islands, the Amazon rainforest, and the Sahara. Today, Tom lives in Bristol, England, with his wife and three children, and can be found mostly in the attic.

The Illustrator

Vladimir Jevtic was born and lives in the Republic of Serbia. In 2015, he graduated in illustration and book design from the Faculty of Applied Arts at Belgrade's University of Arts. He followed up with a Master's in academic studies in 2016. During these years, Vladimir drew caricatures and illustrations for the popular Serbian weekly magazine *Politikin Zabavnik*. He has also illustrated the children's books *You Can't Go In* (2016) and *Ola the Ostrich* (2017).

Picture Credits (abbreviations: t = top; b = bottom; c = center; l = left; r = right)
© www.shutterstock.com:

1 c, 2 cl, 3 c, 4 c, 5 b, 6 t, 6 b, 7 t, 7 b, 11 c, 13 c, 15 c, 17 c, 19 c, 21 c, 23 c, 25 c, 27 c, 28 tr, 28 bl, 29 t, 29 br, 29 tr, 29 cl, 29 br, 31 cr, 32r.

9 c Doug Perrine / Alamy Stock Photo

Every effort has been made to trace the copyright holders, and we acknowledge in advance for any unintentional omissions. We would be pleased to insert the appropriate acknowledgements in any subsequent edition of this publication.